TECH IN THE TRENCHES

Strategic Inventions of the Crusades

Andrew Coddington

Cavendish Square
New York

Published in 2017 by Cavendish Square Publishing, LLC
243 5th Avenue, Suite 136, New York, NY 10016

First Edition

Website: cavendishsq.com

CPSIA Compliance Information: Batch #CW17CSQ

Library of Congress Cataloging-in-Publication Data

Names: Coddington, Andrew.
Title: Strategic Inventions of the Crusades / Andrew Coddington.
Description: New York : Cavendish Square, 2017. | Series: Series: Tech in the trenches | Includes index.
Identifiers: ISBN 9781502623539 (library bound) | ISBN 9781502623546 (ebook)
Subjects: LCSH: Crusades--Juvenile literature. | Civilization, Medieval--Juvenile literature.
Classification: LCC D157.C63 2017 | DDC 909.07--dc23

Editorial Director: David McNamara
Editor: Kristen Susienka
Copy Editor: Nathan Heidelberger
Associate Art Director: Amy Greenan
Designer: Jessica Nevins
Production Coordinator: Karol Szymczuk
Photo Researcher: J8 Media

The photographs in this book are used by permission and through the courtesy of: Cover, p. 1 Sgt. Ethan E. Rocke/File:Modular Tactical Vest Okinawa.jpg/Wikimedia Commons; p. 4 Simon Evans/The National Library of Wales http://www.llgc.org.uk/File: Siege and destruction of Jerusalem (f. 155v) Cropped.jpg/Wikimedia Commons (Public Domain); p. 7 Renewer/Shutterstock.com; p. 8 © Classic Image/Alamy Stock Photo; p. 12 DEA Picture Library/De Agostini Picture Library/Getty Images; p. 15 Universal History Archive/Universal Images Group/Getty Images; p. 19 Ullstein Bild/Getty Images; p. 26 Chris Hellier/Corbis Documentary/Getty Images; p. 29 Ira Block/National Geographic Magazines/Getty Images; p. 33 ZU_09/E+/Getty Images; pp. 36-37 Jean de Courcy/Getty Images; p. 38 Leemage/Universal Images Group/Getty Images; p. 42 Worcester Art Museum, Massachusetts, USA/Bridgeman Images; p. 49 Fine Art Images/Heritage Images/Getty Images; p. 51 DEA/C. Balossini/De Agostini/Getty Images; p. 54 Kachelhoffer Clement/Corbis Historical/Getty Images; p. 56 Private Collection/The Stapleton Collection/Bridgeman Images; pp. 62-63 Martchan/Shutterstock.com; p. 66 Bibliotheque Municipale de Lyon, France/Bridgeman Images; pp. 70-71 Morphart Creation/Shutterstock.com; p. 73 grafvision/Shutterstock.com; p. 76 Luxerendering/Shutterstock.com; p. 80 Florilegius/SSPL/Getty Images; p. 88, 94-95 Buyenlarge/Archive Photos/Getty Images; p. 97 JACK GUEZ/AFP/Getty Images; p. 99 Joi (http://www.flickr.com/photos/joi/)http://www.flickr.com/photos/joi/5594849986/in/set-72157626440197508/File: Neptunic shark suit.jpg /Wikimedia Commons (Creative Commons Attribution 2.0 Generic license).

Printed in the United States of America

CONTENTS

The Crusades were a series of wars fought between the Latin Christian West and the Muslim East.

Holy War

In the eleventh century CE, Pope Urban II, the leader of **Latin Christianity** situated primarily in western and central Europe, made an unprecedented speech to an outdoor gathering of the faithful in Clermont, France. There he summoned Christians everywhere to spend years traveling thousands of miles to fight in the **Holy Land**, a corner of the world so named because of its ties to the ministry, life, and death of Jesus Christ, the central figure of the Christian religion. The sacred sites where Jesus had preached, died, and been resurrected—especially Jerusalem—Urban said, were now controlled by **infidels**, followers of a religion known as **Islam**, which threatened Christianity. Ironically, for a religion based on a man whose teachings included a number of calls to pacifism, the Christian West listened to the pope's call and mobilized thousands to conquer in the name of religion.

Urban's call started the first of a number of wars fought between Latin Christians and Muslims for control of the Holy Land. This period was known as the **Crusades**. Unknown—or perhaps overlooked—by the Latin Christians was the fact that Islam also had religious ties to the very sites that Christians worried were under attack. In response to the Christian threat, Muslims fought back, no less convinced that their war with the Christian West, their **jihad**, or "struggle," to establish Islam as the dominant religion, was no less pious, no less ordained by God. For nearly two hundred years, both sides fought, convinced that they and not their enemy were the agents of God's will.

The Crusades were characterized in part by the synthesis of new military technology, strategies, and architecture as part of the cultural exchange that accompanied the clash between East and West. As the Crusaders and Muslims met one another in battle, they adapted to their opponent's tactics and weapons. Occasionally, they adopted for themselves those methods that proved successful for their enemy. In general, these developments centered around heavily fortified points of fixed defenses, including especially the city of Jerusalem.

Throughout history, people have interpreted the Crusades in various ways. To some, the Crusades were the quintessential examples of the sort of brutality that accompanies militant religious belief, while others point to periods of the Crusades' history when

Jerusalem, in modern-day Israel, contains many sites with religious significance, such as Islam's Dome of the Rock, pictured above. Control of the city was the objective of the Crusades.

either chivalrous Christian knights or noble Muslim warriors fought bravely against their barbaric enemies. Some argue that the Crusades were unprovoked wars of aggression on the part of power-hungry Westerners, while others justify them as attempts to reclaim territory lost to Muslim expansionists and defend those Christians living under Muslim rule. Historically, the Crusades lasted for nearly two hundred years and may contain instances where all of those statements bear weight. The Crusades present a controversial chapter in the history of Christianity and Islam, and the conflicts that stemmed from that clash of cultures continue even today.

In the eleventh century, Pope Urban II called for the First Crusade at the Council of Clermont, saying, "God wills it!"

CHAPTER ONE

The Context of the Crusades

The Crusades were prefaced by a number of complex historical, political, religious, and economic circumstances, which had been in flux for centuries. By the turn of the tenth century CE, there arose two dynamic cultures that seemed destined to come into conflict: Latin Christendom in the West and the Muslim world in the East. By the time of the Crusades, both had determined that it was not only permissible but necessary and just to wage war in the name of God.

CHRISTIANITY

The West, which is commonly accepted by historians to include especially western and central Europe, was defined by two seismic cultural shifts that signaled the start of a period of history known as the Middle Ages. In the fourth century CE, the Roman emperor Constantine the Great worked to make Christianity, once a persecuted eastern cult that preached the divinity of an executed religious and political rebel named Jesus Christ, the official religion of the Roman Empire. Although Christianity had found a sizable following in the Roman Empire, especially in major urban centers situated around the Mediterranean, the institutional legitimacy Constantine granted to the religion made it the dominant religion in practically every corner of the empire. By the Middle Ages, a form of Christianity called Latin Christianity (today known as Roman Catholicism), so called after its language and culture, had been adopted almost universally across Europe.

The second cultural shift that initiated the Middle Ages was the slow decline and eventual erosion of Rome's control over the western half of its empire. Following a series of attacks by barbarian tribes from eastern Europe and central Asia, the city of Rome ultimately fell under the command of a Germanic military officer named Odoacer in 476 CE. Although historians disagree on when the Roman Empire "collapsed" (the eastern half of the empire, operating out of Constantinople in modern-day Turkey, survived largely intact as the Byzantine Empire until 1453), most agree that Europe was fundamentally changed after this exchange of power.

In the wake of the Roman Empire, much of Europe fell into cultural darkness. The benefits of civilization, including high culture, organized government, and military protection, that

Rome had provided now eroded, and much of the West was left to its own devices as barbarian tribes battled for control of the scraps of the empire. In 500 CE, one tribe, the Franks, seized control of a large area of land in western Europe, giving rise to the modern country of France. In 800 CE, a Frank named Charlemagne expanded his control to include France, Germany, and Italy, ushering in a brief period of imperial control. After the death of Charlemagne and his descendants, known as the Carolingians, Europe again fell into violent disarray, as rivals within the empire fought one another for control while barbarian raiders, particularly Viking northerners, picked away from the outside. Throughout this time, however, the Latin Church persisted, maintaining some semblance of order and common culture in the fractured West.

THE DARK AGES

In the wake of the Roman and Carolingian Empires, Latin Christendom seemed to be in a state of decline. Barbarians continued to wreak havoc on the frontiers of Europe, while numerous wars for succession waged across the continent. The civilized security of those past great empires seemed to be merely a memory of a better time.

By the eleventh century, Europe had stabilized somewhat, though the West's political landscape remained fractured under a system of organization known as **feudalism**. Under feudalism, a landowner distributed land to tenants known as vassals in exchange for loyalty. However, pledged loyalty meant that the lands within a region were only loosely affiliated and controlled by largely independent rulers. While a lord may be "the king's man," he had practically unlimited sway over those lands under his control. A lord's power went largely unchecked, making violence common. Many landholders became warlords and engaged in countless personal conflicts against their rivals.

Adding to this was the fact that much of the West remained wilderness, and mass communications technology, such as the

This detail from the Bayeux Tapestry of the eleventh century demonstrates the primacy of knights in medieval European warfare.

printing press, was not yet invented. These contributed to isolating individual regions from one another. In fact, it was not uncommon for individuals, especially commoners, to live their whole lives without ever traveling more than 50 miles (80 kilometers) from their homes. The rise of violence, lack of social advancement, and general sense of decline has led many historians to refer to the centuries before the Crusades as the Dark Ages.

Those living during this period believed that they were witnessing the last, dark, desperate days of humanity, and **apocalyptic** predictions about the end of the world were common. Although the Europeans of the Middle Ages were several centuries removed from the life and death of Jesus Christ, his prediction that the end of the world was near and would be preceded by an age of suffering, which would include wars, famine, and spiritual darkness, was in the forefront of Christians' minds. At the end would be the Last Judgment, when each soul would be called to account for his thoughts and actions in life. The stakes could not be higher: those deemed unworthy of God's grace would be sentenced to eternal suffering in hell, while the worthy would be saved and enjoy the fruits of heaven. To the Western Christians of the late first millennium, that time had come. Priests began devoting a great deal of their time to reading and interpreting the Book of Revelation, a section of the Christian Bible that prophesies how the world as it is known will conclude and the heavenly kingdom of God will reign. Preachers warning ordinary people about the "end of days" were common. Apocalyptic anxiety came to a head in the first part of the eleventh century, when fears were rampant that the millennial anniversary of Jesus's crucifixion (popularly thought to have happened in 33 CE) would mark the beginning of the end.

Even after 1033 had come and passed without a climactic scorching of the earth, Latins continued to worry about the fate of their souls either after the apocalypse or when they died—whichever would come first. Unlike modern Europeans' inclination toward secularism, the Europeans of the Middle Ages were highly religious, listening intently to what priests and other spiritual guides told them. Sermons worked to inspire fear in listeners, describing the tortures of hell that await the evil and undeserving, which, under the Latin Church's doctrine at the time, included practically everyone. As if that were not enough, religious artwork more often than not depicted spiritual agony and torment in graphic detail. The Western Christians almost universally cried out to the Latin Church for guidance on how to cleanse their souls of sin and thereby save themselves. Many turned to monasticism, a way of life in which an individual would live and work in a community, putting aside earthly pleasures and pledging that he or she would live a life of poverty, chastity, and religious obedience. Unfortunately, monasticism was not practical for many Christians, so other ways to cleanse one's soul were required. Into this anxiety-prone culture stepped a religious leader who offered a sure path to salvation: the pope.

This illumination shows God's angels harassing demons locked in spiritual torment in hell.

THE POPE

The figure responsible for the Crusades in the West was the bishop of Rome, otherwise known as the pope. (The word "pope" comes from the Latin word for dad, which is *papa*, the nickname those who occupied the office of Rome's bishop adopted for themselves.) That the pope convinced tens of thousands of Latin Christians across the West to leave their homes to fight in the Holy Land was a feat in itself, for by no means was the pope the only leader of the Christian Church, nor was he the strongest or the most authoritative. Ever since Christianity began its westward spread, it was traditionally held that there were five leaders, called patriarchs, of the faith. These included the bishop of Rome as well as the bishops of four other key urban centers around the Mediterranean: Constantinople, Antioch, Jerusalem, and Alexandria. The political fragmentation and isolation that shaped the secular landscape in Europe in the wake of the Roman Empire's collapse was also keenly felt in the Christian Church. Just as regions of the West enjoyed autonomy during the Middle Ages, the patriarchs also exerted influence over their own dominions—although with varying success. Even in the eleventh century, the pope, situated at the center of the collapse of the Roman Empire, struggled to control his own corner of central Italy, let alone Western Christendom as a whole. Occasionally, the pope was even expelled from Rome.

Despite the papacy's tenuous control, it nevertheless sought to establish itself as the ultimate authority over Christendom and every aspect of life of those living within it. In the mid-eleventh century, the papacy embarked on the so-called Reform movement to realize this end. In the pope's mind, the decline of the West—politically, socially, and morally—stemmed from centuries of power sharing between kings and the Latin Church. For as much as Constantine did to legitimize Christianity within the Roman Empire in the fourth century, he also set the precedent of secular leaders influencing and even dominating Christian religious affairs. According to the papacy, this secular control over religious matters was responsible for the violence and discord rampant in the West. It could only be remedied by the pope exercising his supreme, God-given authority over all things. Part of that line of reasoning, most strongly advocated by Pope Gregory VII (1073–1085), was that the pope also had the right to summon armies consisting of the faithful from all corners of Christendom, regardless of nationality, to fight in support of God and the Latin Church (at the command of the pope himself).

Although the Crusades went a long way to consolidating papal authority and mobilizing Latin Christians to see the papacy as the primary authority in Europe, the pope was not driven only by political motives. The pope had long believed that he was responsible for his "flock," those Christians who depended on him for spiritual guidance, and that when the time came for the pope himself to be judged, he would be responsible for not only his actions but the actions of all those for whom he was responsible.

With the fate of Latin Christians and the memory of the stability and affluence of the Roman and Carolingian Empires in mind, the pope began mobilizing to restore the West to its former glory. In 1095, Pope Urban II called all those within Latin Christendom to launch a Crusade, a holy war not only to reclaim territory in the Holy Land but also to cleanse the stain of sin on the souls of the Crusaders.

MUHAMMAD AND THE RISE OF ISLAM

While Western Christendom struggled through its dark night of the soul, another culture was developing and expanding in the eastern part of the Mediterranean and northern Africa during the latter half of the first millennium: Islam. Muslims traditionally point to 610 CE as the dawning of their faith. In that year, Muhammad, a middle-aged Arab from Mecca in modern-day Saudi Arabia, was contacted by the archangel Gabriel with messages containing revelations into the nature of the divine from Allah, the Muslim name for the one true God. These revelations were later written down and form the Quran, Islam's holy scripture. Muslims consider Muhammad to be the last of God's prophets and the Quran to be the unadulterated word of God.

Islam shares a similar cultural and theological heritage with Judaism and Christianity, which Muhammad would have certainly been exposed to during his lifetime. For example, Arab Muslims believe that they are descended from the Jewish patriarch Abraham; however, unlike Jews, who draw their lineage from

This sixteenth-century Turkish reproduction of a manuscript illustrates Muhammad's inspiration from Allah.

Abraham's wife, Sarah, and her son, Isaac, Muslims believe they are descended from Hagar, Abraham's concubine, and her son, Ishmael. Muhammad himself considered Abraham, Moses, and even Jesus Christ to be lesser prophets within the Muslim faith. However, Muslims believe Muhammad's revelations fulfill and perfect Judaism and Christianity.

Inspired by his revelations and armed with the conviction that Islam (meaning "submission to the will of God") was the progressive refinement of the other major world religions, Muhammad began preaching in Mecca and the surrounding area in an effort to convert his polytheistic countrymen. The pagan Arabs were not pleased with Muhammad's message, and in 622 the Prophet fled from Mecca to the nearby city of Medina, where he had much greater success in gathering converts to the new faith. Shortly after arriving in Medina, Muhammad led his followers in a years-long war against Mecca, which eventually fell to the Muslims.

Muhammad died in 632, but Islam's march of conquest did not end with Mecca. The Quran makes a clear call to the faithful to spread Islamic faith and law to every corner of the world. The tribes of the Arabian Peninsula, united under their common faith and led by a series of militarily savvy **caliphs** (successors to Muhammad), started a campaign across the Near East. Just decades after Muhammad's death, the Muslim state included the Arabian Peninsula as well as Palestine, Syria, Iraq, and Egypt. By the mid-eighth century, Islam controlled as far east as the Indus River and western China and as far west as North Africa, Spain, and parts of France. Indeed, Islam may have spread clear across Europe if it were not twice foiled in the capture of Constantinople in the East and ultimately driven back at Poitiers in the West by the Frankish king Charles the Hammer.

Like the Roman Empire, the Muslims did not require all conquered peoples to convert to the religion of the victors; Christians and Jews, whom the early Muslims called "People of the Book" who followed a similar (albeit incomplete, outdated, and misguided) version of Islam, were permitted to practice their faith in exchange for a tax.

THE MUSLIM WORLD BEFORE THE CRUSADES

While Islam's meteoric sweep across much of western Asia, North Africa, and parts of Europe might suggest a concerted and unified base of support, cracks had started to form during this period of expansion. In 661, the last of a line of Muhammad's descendants, known as the "Rightly Guided Caliphs," ended with the death of Muhammad's cousin and son-in-law. A sect of Islam, known as Shiat Ali ("Party of Ali"), or Shia for short, broke off from the mainstream Sunni ("tradition") sect. According to the Shiites, only descendants of Ali and his wife Fatima, who was also Muhammad's daughter, have a rightful claim to the caliphate. As the two groups continued to diverge, they developed unique approaches to the practice of the faith.

For the next several centuries, political dynasties within the Muslim world rose to prominence, shifting the center of power and, thus, the evolution of Islam as they did so. The first of these clans was the Umayyads, who in the mid-seventh century moved the capital of Islam out of Arabia to Damascus, Syria. The Umayyads were overthrown in 750 by another dynasty known as the Abbasids, who removed the capital to Iraq, where they built the city of Baghdad. Situated in Mesopotamia, the so-called "cradle of civilization," the caliphate in Baghdad sponsored the advancement of science, philosophy, and technology.

However, the rise of the Abbasids signaled the fracturing of the Muslim empire. In the eighth century, Spanish Muslims known as the Moors broke off to form an independent nation, and in the tenth century, a fractious Shiite group known as the Fatimids gained dominance in North Africa and organized their own caliph to rival the Sunni one situated in Baghdad. Throughout this period, the power vested in the leaders of each dynasty waned and, as in Europe, meaningful power came to be wielded by regional lords, such as the Iraqi sultan and the Egyptian vizier.

In the early eleventh century, a warlike nomadic tribe from central Asia known as the Turks began migrating into the Islamic world. A faction of Turks known as the Seljuqs adopted Sunni Islam and swore allegiance the Abbasid caliphate. In 1055, a Seljuq warlord became the sultan, or governor, of Baghdad, effectively granting the Turkish immigrants practical political and religious authority. Bolstered by the influx of the aggressive Turks and their ferocious mounted archers, the Abbasids began moving against their religious rivals in the **Levant**, reconquering Damascus and Jerusalem from the Umayyads and gaining large swaths of Fatimid-held territory in North Africa.

Thus, to outside Christian observers in the century leading up to the Crusades, it may have seemed that the Islamic world was a mobilized juggernaut kicking into gear and sweeping closer into Christian Europe. However, in reality, before the Crusades, Muslim politics were nearly as fragmented as those of Christendom. Nevertheless, in 1095, Pope Urban II issued the call for all Christians to make way to the Holy Land in service of their faith.

Jerusalem: The Capital of Conflict

Much of the action of the Crusades focused on the city of Jerusalem. Located in modern-day Israel, Jerusalem has held religious significance for the main religions in the region: Judaism, Christianity, and Islam. This has been the cause of tension, conflict, and bloodshed as each religion has battled for control before losing it to a rival faction, a pattern that was apparent during the Crusades and continues even today.

The first religion to occupy Jerusalem was Judaism. According to chapter 12 in Deuteronomy, one of the books in the Tanakh (Hebrew Bible), Jerusalem was reserved for the Jews by God, "as a place established in His name. It is there you shall go to seek his presence." By the tenth century BCE, when King David brought the **Ark of the Covenant**, Jerusalem had become the Jewish state's religious and political capital. David's son Solomon constructed the Temple, the permanent center for the Jewish religion in Jerusalem, but centuries of invaders led to cycles of destruction and reconstruction of the Temple until the Romans razed it and the rest of the city in 70 CE. Jerusalem and the Temple have nevertheless remained imprinted in the Jewish psyche ever afterward.

Christianity's claim to Jerusalem contains far less history but is no less significant to Christians. Sometime in the late 20s to early 30s CE, Jesus Christ (himself a Jew) traveled to Jerusalem to observe the holiday of Passover. His entry was marked by a procession of followers, who treated him like a conquering hero and exclaimed that the kingdom of God was at hand. Shortly after his arrival, Jesus was arrested by the religious establishment, tried by the Roman prefect in charge, and sentenced to death. Jesus was crucified and buried outside the city limits of Jerusalem, and Christian tradition holds that he was resurrected there three days later. Later Christians marked the spot of Christ's crucifixion and burial with a chapel, known as the **Church of the Holy Sepulchre**, and many medieval Christians believed that Jerusalem was to be the focus of the apocalypse.

Muslims captured the city from the Byzantine Christians in 638, and it became Islam's third-holiest site after Mecca and Medina. Part of the reason for this stems from the fact that Islam, descended from the Jewish patriarch Abraham, shares a similar cultural heritage with Judaism, but the larger reason owes to the belief that Jerusalem was the site where Muhammad ascended to heaven when he died. The site is known as Haram al-Sharif, or the Temple Mount, which now consists of the last standing wall of the Jewish Temple and the Dome of the Rock, the site where Muhammad ascended to heaven. Furthermore, Muslims, much like Christians, also believe in an apocalyptic end of the world and that the religious events that occurred there designate it as the place where it will begin and end.

The First Crusade reached its climax in 1099, when Muslim and Christian forces clashed at Jerusalem.

CHAPTER TWO

Trial by Fire: The First Crusade, 1095–1099

Historians disagree on exactly how many Crusades there were. This is because there were many instances where the Latin Church had summoned Christian armies to fight against Islam only to end in failure, while other "Crusades" were called against **heretical** groups within Europe itself. Generally speaking, there were between seven and nine "true" Crusades that occurred within a two-hundred-year period, with Christian armies under direction from the pope battling Muslim forces for control of key religious sites in the Holy Land. Of these, the first four are considered the "principal Crusades," with the remaining classified as "minor Crusades."

"GOD WILLS IT"

The First Crusade was called for by Pope Urban II at the Council of Clermont, which began on November 18, 1095. While there, Urban, a Frenchman, along with bishops (primarily from southern France), occupied themselves with ecclesiastical business typical of an **ecumenical** council. At the end of Clermont, Urban addressed a large outdoor gathering, where he called for war against the Muslims in the East. Among the reasons the pope cited to support his call to arms was the current conflict between Byzantine Christians under Emperor Alexius I Comnenus and Muslim aggressors, the harassment of Christian pilgrims traveling to holy sites, and the destruction of places within the Holy Land, especially within Jerusalem. To fight in this war, Urban said, would be to willingly endure suffering in service of God and in so doing cleanse one's soul of sin. To this end, Urban suggested that the Crusade would be well served by criminals, who could turn their aggressive tendencies toward the service of God and Christianity. Although the exact text of Urban's speech will never be known, he apparently concluded it with the words "*Deus le volt*" ("God wills it").

Urban's call to arms was received enthusiastically by all manner of Christians, including elites and knights, as well as those in the lower classes of European society. While the wealthy began selling off property and mortgaging their estates to finance the purchase of new equipment and passage to the Holy Land, a popular uprising consisting of peasants began marching across Europe. Known as the People's Crusade, this movement comprised several

Latin Christian forces organized at the city of Constantinople at the mouth of the Bosporus Strait. Once a Christian stronghold in the East, Constantinople eventually fell to the Muslim Ottoman Turks and was renamed Istanbul.

largely disorganized groups. One of these, under the command of a preacher named Peter the Hermit, arrived at Constantinople, the capital of the Byzantine Empire and the staging ground for the First Crusade, well in advance of the main force of Crusaders.

Although encouraged by Emperor Alexius to wait until the main force had arrived, Peter's troops were overeager and traveled into the Holy Land without any support. While en route, the People's Crusade was ambushed by the Turks and decimated before even reaching the Holy Land.

The main Crusader force, known as the Prince's Crusade, arrived at Constantinople in late December 1096, as Urban had expected. All told, the European army consisted of between fifty thousand and sixty thousand soldiers and attendants, seven thousand of which were knights, divided between a coalition of four armies. Of these, only one was led by a German prince, Godfrey of Bouillon; the rest were composed mostly of Frenchmen, a product of Urban's French heritage and the fact that the original call to Crusade was made in France. In fact, French was so common in the First Crusade that the Muslims came to call the Europeans Franks.

In May 1097, a coalition of European Crusaders and Byzantine troops marched toward the Muslim-held city of Antioch, crossing Anatolia in modern-day Turkey. The passage proved difficult for the heavily outfitted Crusaders, considering the mountainous Anatolian peninsula in summer was hot and dry. Adding to this, the Crusaders were under near-constant harassment and threat of attack from Seljuq Turks. On the way, Godfrey's brother Baldwin broke off from the main force and seized control of the county of Edessa, which would serve as a fortified buffer between Muslim encroachment and Constantinople.

CAPTURING ANTIOCH

In October, the Crusaders arrived at Antioch and settled into a long **siege** that lasted until early June 1098. Antioch was heavily fortified to the point that the Crusaders could not penetrate it by force alone, so the fate of the city would go to the side that could survive starvation the longest. The Crusaders' blockade intercepted several attempts to resupply the city, further tightening their grip; however, the Crusaders themselves suffered from a shortage of supplies, and many soldiers died or deserted during the course of the siege. One of these deserters, a French knight named Stephen of Blois, believed the siege was doomed to fail. While heading back to Constantinople, Stephen encountered Emperor Alexius at the head of a column of soldiers marching to reinforce the Crusaders at Antioch. He convinced the emperor that there was no hope for Antioch, and Alexius decided to turn back rather than risk the destruction of his army.

The Crusaders were already threatened by a counterattack led by the Muslim commander Kerbogha of Mosul when word of Alexius's retreat reached them. Feeling betrayed, the Crusaders decided that they would proceed without the condition that their conquests be returned to the emperor. A Norman from Southern France named Bohemond, who wanted the city for himself, took control of the armies and made contact with a watchman within the city walls, who agreed to abandon his post one night and permit the Crusaders to enter the city. That night, the Christians spilled into Antioch, catching the defenders by surprise and seizing control of the entire city, except the fortified **citadel** at the center.

When Kerbogha's army arrived at Antioch, the Crusaders managed to resist the Muslim attempt to retake the city. Afterward, the Christian commanders were split on what to do with the city: Bohemond, who orchestrated its capture, believed he had claim to the city; Raymond of Saint-Gilles, the head of the largest army within the coalition, believed that it should be returned to the Byzantines as previously agreed. The argument stalled the progress of the war, and only when the soldiers under Bohemond and Raymond's command threatened to riot and raze the city did the two reluctantly continue their march south through the Holy Land.

Indicating the degree to which the Islamic world was politically and religiously fractured during the Crusades, the Shiite Fatimids in Egypt, an Islamic sect that rivaled the Sunni Seljuqs in the Levant, entered into negotiations with the Crusaders around this time to facilitate the Christians' capture of other cities along the way to Jerusalem. Fatimid support destabilized the Seljuqs in the Levant, and a Fatimid army under the command of the vizier al-Afdal swept into Seljuq territory and captured Jerusalem. A dispatch of Crusader delegates met with al-Afdal to negotiate a settlement in which the Christians would hand over a section of their newly won territory in exchange for access to Jerusalem; however, the Fatimids refused the offer outright. The Crusaders hastily turned toward Jerusalem in hopes of seizing it for themselves.

The four commanders of the First Crusade (*left to right*): Godfrey of Bouillon, Raymond of Saint-Gilles, Bohemond, and Tancred of Hauteville

THE SIEGE OF JERUSALEM

In June 1099, the Crusader coalition, now reduced to approximately fifteen thousand troops as a result of casualties in battle, starvation, disease, and desertion, reached the Holy City, the object of a war that spanned 2,000 miles (3,218 km) and nearly four years. Unlike at Antioch, the Crusaders could not cut off Jerusalem from its supply routes, as the city was too vast. Complicating matters was the fact that the army had marched with haste to the city without taking time to set up supply lines or even secure an escape route. The only way to capture the Holy City—to survive the expedition at all—would be to penetrate the city's defenses before Muslim reinforcements arrived.

Though al-Afdal's army had not yet arrived to organize Jerusalem's defense, capturing the city would be no easy task. Jerusalem stood between three deep valleys to the east, southeast, and west that thwarted direct attack, and the city itself was surrounded by 2.5 miles (4 km) of walls that were 60 feet (18 meters) high and 10 feet (3 m) thick. The north and south, the only paths open to viable assault, were protected by a secondary wall and ditches. In the west and northwest, meanwhile, stood two formidable fortresses, the Tower of David and the Quadrangular Tower. Jerusalem's governor, Iftikhar ad-Daulah, had also been actively preparing to defend the city. Leading up to the Crusaders' approach, ad-Daulah had ravaged the surrounding countryside, poisoning wells and chopping down trees. By the time the Crusaders arrived, there was hardly any freshwater to drink or lumber to burn for fuel or to build shelters or **siege engines**. Fearing that Jerusalem would also fall not by strength of arms but sedition from within, as in the case of Antioch, ad-Daulah also expelled many of the city's eastern Christians for fear they might sympathize with the Crusaders and grant access to the city.

Since Antioch, infighting among the Crusader coalition had grown, and at Jerusalem, Raymond and Godfrey, the two most powerful commanders, split their forces. Raymond occupied Mount Zion to the southwest and Godfrey mobilized his forces to attack from the north. The two forces only had one scaling ladder between them with which to mount an attack. On June 13, encouraged by prophecies from a Christian hermit living nearby, the armies launched their first attempt to scale Jerusalem's walls. The Latins charged forward, managing to lift their ladder and scrambling to reach the ramparts; however, as soon as the first man grabbed hold of the wall, a Muslim cut his hand off with a sword, and the Crusaders were forced to fall back.

The Latin commanders decided to wait to stage another assault on the fortress until the proper siege engines could be constructed, which proved easier said than done in the barren countryside. Meanwhile, the summer heat of the Near East began taking its toll on the Europeans. The search for water became paramount, and many took to drinking filthy water collected from sources contaminated with bacteria and, at one point, leeches. Thus, many Crusaders occasionally postponed dehydration only to later die of infection.

The Crusaders' prospects changed dramatically in mid-June when a flotilla of supply ships from Genoa, Italy, anchored at Jaffa, a natural harbor near Jerusalem, bearing supplies and craftsmen. The Crusaders also received intelligence about forests within marching distance of the camp and quickly began moving timber to build siege engines. As the Crusaders went to work building the weapons needed to make a more robust assault on the city, both sides took time to humiliate and antagonize each other. Several times the Muslims dragged crosses to the top of the city walls, spitting and sometimes urinating on them in full view of the encamped Christians; the Christians, for their part, took to publicly executing captured Muslim soldiers.

Once the Crusaders overcame Jerusalem's defenses, they embarked on a campaign of pillaging, torture, and murder.

The Crusaders finished building their machines of war by mid-July 1099, and on the morning of July 14, they launched a sneak attack. For weeks, Godfrey's forces had been building a massive siege tower in front of the Quadrangular Tower, which the Muslims diligently reinforced in preparation for an attack. Overnight, however, Godfrey's men deconstructed the specially designed tower in sections, relocated it, and reassembled it in the less protected northwest corner of the city. On the other side,

This is a nineteenth-century portrait of Godfrey of Bouillon.

Raymond's forces also maneuvered a siege tower into position after spending weeks filling in the dry moat at the south of the city with rocks. The two fronts divided the defenders' attention, and the following day, Godfrey's tower reached the wall. The Crusaders swarmed over the top, and the Muslim defenders retreated in fright.

By midday on July 15, the Crusaders had conquered the city. Met with little resistance, the Crusaders coursed through the city. What followed was perhaps the darkest moment in the history of the Crusades, as the soldiers of the Latin Church's Holy War proceeded to loot and massacre the citizens—Muslims, Jews, and Christians—men, women, and children alike. A chronicler reports that people were tortured, beheaded, and burned to death, and their bodies were desecrated in cold blood. Modern historians estimate that between three thousand and ten thousand people were killed.

It is significant that the two most important battles of the First Crusade centered on the capture of heavily fortified cities. Each served as the locus of control for its respective region. Success in warfare during the Crusades hinged on the importance of the fortress and an army's ability to keep or take it. Reflecting this reality, the Crusades made advancements in three fields of warfare: the use of battlefield tactics centered around cavalry in fighting outside the fortress, the improvement of the designs and materials used in fortifications, and the development of more powerful siege engines to topple the strongest of defenses.

The Knights Templar

With the success of the First Crusade, Christians began flocking to the Holy Land for pilgrimages. However, with the end of open conflict, many of the Crusaders returned home, leaving new states too weak to protect themselves from intermittent Muslim raids. Individual pilgrims often fell victim to robbery and murder on their way to the holy sites.

Around 1119, a French knight called Hugh de Payns collected a small band of other knights and formed a religious community to protect the newly won territories in the Holy Land. They called themselves the Poor Knights of Christ or the Knights Templar.

Although the chief goal of the Knights Templar was military protection for pilgrims, de Payns structured the Templars after a religious order of Christian monks known as the Benedictines. Each Templar made vows of poverty, chastity, and obedience, as monks had. Likewise, the knights' daily lives mirrored life in a monastery, with regimented times reserved for prayers and mass, the expectation that the knights would observe fasts and vigils, and the requirement that the knights live in community. However, unlike monks, the Templars commanded forts, garrisoned towns, and fielded forces in battle against Muslims in succeeding Crusades.

Ironically, considering the Templar vow of poverty, the Templars amassed enormous wealth and power during their nearly three centuries of operation. Initially, de Payns petitioned European kings, clerics, and nobles for financial support to grow the order and fund their operations. Over time, the Templars were handed fortresses, fortunes, and favors by a number of European elites, including even the pope. In 1139, Pope Innocent II declared that the Templars would not be required to pay a tithe (church tax) and would be subject to the pope's authority alone, granting the order exceptional powers to self-govern. Over time, the order swelled in size and enjoyed considerable influence in not only the Holy Land but Europe itself.

Eventually, the Templars' power and influence turned sour. In 1307, King Philip IV of France ordered the arrest of every Templar in his country and all their property seized. At Philip's urging, Pope Clement V (also a Frenchman) embarked on a policy of suppression of the Templars, whom he argued were a heretical order. In 1312, Clement authorized a rival order of knights known as the Hospitallers as well as government bodies to confiscate Templar-held property throughout Europe. The Templars were arrested, and many were tortured. Those that confessed to heresy were permitted to retire within the Hospitallers, but those that refused, including the Knights' grand master, Jacques de Molay, were sent to trial. Those found guilty were sentenced to life imprisonment. When de Molay protested, he was burned at the stake.

Mounted soldiers played an important role in both Christian and Muslim armies during the Crusades.

CHAPTER THREE

Cavalry in the Crusades

Warfare during the Crusades was partly characterized by the presence of a large number of mounted warriors in both Christian and Muslim armies. Although horses had been used in warfare for millennia, the Crusades saw a number of advancements in cavalry technology and tactics.

THE ARMIES OF THE ANCIENT WORLD

Save for some notable exceptions, the primary fighting force for practically every ancient military was infantry. The ancient Greeks pioneered foot soldier–based fighting tactics with the development of hoplite, or heavily armored, warriors and their fighting style, known as the phalanx. Each hoplite was protected by a bronze helmet, greaves (shin guards), and occasionally a chest plate. Hoplites also carried short swords, but the most essential gear was a round shield and a 6-foot (1.8 m) thrusting spear, which was brought to full effect in the phalanx formation. Hoplites would organize the phalanx formation by standing side by side in a row, with several more rows—usually eight—behind the front line. Each soldier's shield would cover half of himself as well as half of the soldier next to him, and so on down the line. Acting together, the hoplites, protected by each other's shields, would march toward their target, thrusting their spears in unison into the enemy line. Should one warrior in the front line fall in battle, the man behind him would step forward and again complete the unit.

The hoplites' heavy armor and disciplined phalanx tactics made them a force to be reckoned with in the ancient world. Until that point, ancient armies had largely been accustomed to battles decided by either a series of duels between individual "heroes," such as those described in Homer's *Iliad*, or chaotic, undisciplined skirmishes in which victory went to the side that had brought the largest force to the battle. What the bronze-clad hoplites lacked in maneuverability or individual fighting talent the phalanx made up for in sheer mass. As a phalanx slowly marched toward the enemy, it presented a solid wall of shields and raised spears, resistant to arrows, slung rocks, or other ranged ballistic attacks. The weight of the phalanx proved the hoplites' deadliest asset, as their force slammed into the enemy and ultimately broke through the lines.

The phalanx formation also meant that numbers no longer decided the battle. In August 480 BCE, a small Greek coalition, led by the Spartan king Leonidas, held off an overwhelmingly large force of Persians at Thermopylae. The Greek warriors formed a phalanx in a narrow mountain pass, withstanding countless waves of Persians until the invaders outflanked the Greeks by maneuvering around a hidden path through the mountains.

Thanks to their heavy infantry, the Greeks quickly became the dominant fighting force in the Mediterranean, and most other civilizations adopted some version of the phalanx for their own armies. Even the ancient Romans, whose unprecedented empire hinged on the strength of their armies, adopted the phalanx, improving on the Greek tactic by incorporating several volleys of throwing spears on approach to an enemy line, short swords for thrusting at close range, and tall, curved shields that completely protected an individual soldier.

THE FALL OF THE FOOT SOLDIER

Heavy infantry was the preferred military unit of choice for ancient armies for centuries, but it did have its limitations. For one, the phalanx required strict discipline among its ranks in order to effectively bring the whole of its weight onto its opponent; if one soldier or one line got overeager and marched ahead of its comrades, or if those men panicked during battle and broke rank, the whole phalanx would implode. Additionally, the phalanx was only effective on its front side, where the shields and spears were facing, but its flanks were completely exposed. This was an acceptable tradeoff in a pitched battle in which two forces marched toward each other, but in battles where a force could somehow maneuver around the phalanx, such as at Thermopylae, the hoplites did not stand a chance.

When the Macedonian king Alexander the Great began his campaign of conquest across the eastern Mediterranean in the 300s BCE, he incorporated the phalanx into his own armies while also exploiting its weaknesses. Alexander the Great's army also included a not-so-secret weapon: cavalry. Known as *hetairoi* or "companion" cavalry, these mounted soldiers were faster and more maneuverable than infantry units, capable of outflanking enemy lines. Thus, in Alexander's army, the phalanx would keep the enemy infantry occupied while the hetairoi situated on the flanks would sweep around and behind the enemy, who could either disperse and lose the force of their combined weight or else get trampled.

THE RISE OF THE KNIGHT IN THE WEST

The advantages of reach, height, speed, maneuverability, and power often made the cavalry the decisive element in battle. However, cavalry, like infantry, was not without its limitations. The costs associated with outfitting and maintaining cavalry were astronomical. For one, the horses themselves were expensive to purchase and keep, requiring feed, water, housing, horseshoes, training, and the oversight of a dedicated caretaker. (Adding to this expense was the fact that horses often died in battle.)

Likewise, the mounted soldier himself was expensive to outfit and also required valets to dress him for battle.

Because of these costs, the cavalry was usually made up of a small number of aristocratic individuals with the resources to afford it. In medieval Europe, this was both a cause and a product of the emergence of a class hierarchy known as feudalism. Under the feudal system, land was the primary source of wealth and power, and those that controlled the land, the landowners, divided it among lower classes, the vassals, in exchange for loyalty and service. The king naturally sat at the top of the system, controlling all land and all those under him. He distributed parcels of his land, known as fiefs, to nobles, known as lords, in exchange for loyalty and military service. Likewise, these lords distributed portions of land to professional warriors, on whom the lords depended to fulfill their military obligations to the king. These warriors, called knights, could afford to pay the expenses associated with outfitting a warhorse because they, in turn, leased their land to peasant farmers, called serfs. Because the knight owned the land, he also owned the product of the serf's labor, while the serfs depended on the knight for food, shelter, and protection. Muslims had a similar system around the time of the Crusades, in which the sultan distributed land or wealth, known as *iqta*, to emirs in exchange for military service.

The feudal construct operated in Europe until about the seventeenth century, when society had developed to a point where monarchs and other governments could effectively govern larger territories centrally rather than relying on lower strata of de facto rulers to oversee sections of the nation. (In fact, relics of the feudal system, such lords and knights, exist in parts of Europe such as England today, though those titles are more honorific than practical.) The Crusades occurred at the height of the feudal system, and those classes that enjoyed the benefits of landownership grew wealthy as a result.

It was the newly emerging class of professional mounted warriors that the Latin Church sought to recruit to join the Crusades. Practically every knight traveled with a contingent of four or five additional servants who looked after their master's horse, equipment, health, and security, but who were also themselves capable foot soldiers. Because the crusading armies lacked the regimentation and command of a standing army, being composed of volunteers expecting to serve only a few months out of the year before returning home, success in open battle depended on the presence of as many fighters as possible.

CAVALRY EQUIPMENT

Because most Crusader armies consisted of volunteers, those that fought could outfit themselves as lavishly as they pleased—the only limit was what a man could afford to spend on his expedition to the Holy Land. Despite this, however, most Christian knights during the Crusades were outfitted in generally the same way. Of course, a knight's most important equipment—the thing that made him a knight—was his horse. Horses during the Middle Ages were typically classified by their use. Those that were used in battle were known as chargers. Chargers were generally taller

Cavalry units were expensive to outfit and equip in part because horses were costly and frequently died in battle.

than other horse breeds, making them strong and fast, and they were specially trained to be agile in battle. The most sought-after European warhorses came from Spain and likely descended from Muslim Barbary and Arabian stocks. A knight also owned another, smaller riding horse, known as a palfrey, for travel, as well as a packhorse to carry his equipment.

In addition to his horse, a knight's other important equipment was his armor. A Crusader's first line of defense consisted mostly of **mail**, or chain mail. The word "mail" comes from the French word *maille,* meaning mesh or net, reflecting the unique pattern of intricate, interlocking metal rings used to create it. Mail was typically crafted of iron or steel. A knight's first piece of mail was usually a shirt or jacket designed to protect the arms and torso, especially the lungs, heart, and intestines. A shirt that reached to a knight's knees or thighs was called a hauberk and might extend to either the elbow or the wrist. The hauberk was split from the crotch down on both the front and back to allow the knight to mount a horse. Beneath the hauberk, a Crusader might wear a padded leather or canvas undershirt. If a knight could afford it, he might also wear mail gloves (*mitons*), leggings (*chausses*), and a hood (*coif*) or collar (*pixane*) to complete his ensemble.

Mail armor provided significant protection from slashing and piercing attacks, such as from arrows and swords. However, mail's flexibility meant that a blow from a hammer or mace or even a powerful sword slash could inflict bruising, break bones, or cause other internal injuries. Occasionally, if individual rings were

The great helm (also known as the barrel or bucket helm) offered improved protection over the nasal helm for knights but sacrificed field of vision and ventilation.

not riveted shut or were made poorly, a slash or jab could break through. Archers also incorporated narrow arrowheads known as bodkins, which were designed to be thin enough to penetrate through the space between the rings of mail. Archaeological evidence suggests that most warriors tried to get around an opponent's mail armor rather than fighting to break through it. An analysis of knights' bodies from Sweden shows most wounds were found on the less well protected legs. After the Crusades, mail armor was improved by adding solid plate armor at strategic locations, and full suits of plate armor eventually replaced mail armor by about the fifteenth century.

In addition to mail, crusading knights also wore a helm or helmet, which protected the head and part or all of the face. There were two common varieties of helmets during the Crusades. The first is the nasal helm, which was the older of the two designs, appearing in Europe during the late ninth century. It featured a metal skullcap with either a domed or pointed top, as well as a strip of metal extending from the brow and covering the nose for additional face protection. By the end of the twelfth century, the nasal helm was replaced by the great helm. Also known as the bucket or barrel helm, the great helm resembles a flat-topped cylinder with small slits or holes for the eyes and mouth. Knights preferred this because it offered much greater face protection than the nasal helm. However, the great helm severely limited the wearer's ventilation and field of vision. During the Crusades, the nasal helm continued to be popular among archers, whose accuracy depended on their eyesight.

Knights also carried a shield, which was generally kite shaped, for additional protection, as well as a personal hand weapon, such as a mace (a heavy, usually pointed ball attached to a handle), a flail (a mace whose head is attached by a length of chain), an axe, a dagger, or especially a sword, which became a symbol of knighthood. Knights also carried a lance, which was used during wide-scale cavalry charges to devastating effect.

MUSLIM CAVALRY

Muslim armies also benefited from having cavalry in their ranks. Muslim cavalry during the Crusades was inspired by the equipment and tactics of the Seljuq Turks that had raided much of the Near East centuries before. Unlike the heavy cavalry of the Christians, the main cavalry unit was a lightly armored warrior riding a smaller, more maneuverable pony. Their main weapon was a light bow, which allowed them to quickly fire short-range volleys of arrows while moving. These warriors also carried a small lance, a single-edged curved sword known as a scimitar, an axe, or a dagger. Muslim armies still employed heavy cavalry similar to Crusader knights, but these were often held in reserve, waiting until an enemy had broken and was in retreat before running them down.

Muslim cavalry tactics also differed from those of the Christians. Whereas the Christians positioned their knights to deliver a single powerful charge in the hopes of shocking their opponents into retreat, Muslim cavalry units sought to cause confusion among their enemy. Their quicker horses and their ability to attack at range allowed them to target the weakest parts of an opposing army. Muslim cavalry archers typically surrounded their opponent on all sides, loosing arrows into the trapped forces of the enemy, who did not know which direction to lead an attack. Another common tactic was feigned retreat, in which the archers would briefly harass the enemy from afar before withdrawing. This often caused the opposing forces to chase after them, breaking their formations and leaving them open to counterattack. Sometimes, feigned retreat could last for days, tiring out the Muslims' pursuers while allowing Muslim forces to dictate the location and timing of a larger assault.

This drawing shows Crusaders attacking the city of Tarsus and battling the Seljuqs in 1097.

The Stirrup

Both Muslim and Christian forces in the Crusades benefited from a technological development that had reached the western half of Eurasia only recently: the **stirrup**. Considered to be one of the greatest advances in military technology prior to the invention of gunpowder, the stirrup dramatically improved the effectiveness of mounted soldiers and contributed to the rise of the heavily armored knight in Europe. Stirrups consist of a pair of loops or frames designed to hold a horseman's feet. These loops are attached to either side of a saddle by straps. Stirrups are used to aid in the mounting of a horse and also greatly improve a rider's ability to stay in the saddle and control the horse.

Evidence of single-stirrup setups, thought to be used exclusively as a mounting aid, has been found in India in the early centuries BCE. Paired stirrups (still in use today) date back to fourth-century-CE China. The technology became popular in Asia and was eventually introduced to central Europe by invading nomadic tribes sometime during the sixth or seventh centuries.

Although the stirrup benefited agriculture, communications, and every other facet of human culture in which horses have been used, the technology's most significant impact lay in warfare. The stirrup improved a rider's ability to control his horse and allowed cavalry forces to apply greater force with their weapons, leveraging both their own strength as well as that of their mount in a devastating charge.

By the time of the Crusades, Jerusalem had been inhabited for centuries. When the Christians arrived, it was a mazelike fortress of concentric walls, citadels, and towers.

CHAPTER FOUR

The Fortress

Despite the supremacy of cavalry on the battlefield, there were few pitched battles during the Crusades. The rise of feudalism meant that most wars were fought between regional rulers, who could only muster small numbers of professional warriors who had pledged their loyalty. Gone were the days of well-funded ancient militaries fielding huge numbers of trained soldiers. As a result of this change, Europe in the Middle Ages transitioned to relying on stationary fortifications designed to repel invaders to maintain hold over the surrounding territory. This shift manifested in the Crusades, where the armies battled in and around fortified cities, castles, and outposts to secure control of the Holy Land. Victory often went to the side that developed and implemented the strongest defenses and the deadliest traps designed to repel assaults.

FORTIFICATIONS BEFORE THE CRUSADES

As with most technological developments in Europe and the Mediterranean during the Middle Ages, the roots of Crusade-era fortification lie in the designs and techniques of the ancient Roman Empire. Much of the earliest Roman fortifications were frontier outposts that were initially constructed to garrison troops during campaigns of expansion. The soldiers themselves usually built these camps, which were square shaped, first digging a defensive trench around the perimeter, piling the dirt on the inside. A wooden fence known as a palisade was built on the mound. The mound also served as a raised walkway that afforded sentries a slight height advantage. Gates were installed on each side and watchtowers situated along the walls.

In the third century CE, when expansion slowed and the need for defensive positions outweighed Rome's ability to garrison large numbers of soldiers on the frontier, these camps were incorporated into a network of forts with more complicated ditch systems, known as limites (singular limes). These limites included a series of ditches filled with branches, brambles, and water, as well as a deep earthen wall. They also incorporated traps, such as ***stimuli*** and ***lilia***. The limites were designed to both deter an attack as well as slow an enemy's assault long enough that they either gave up or fell prey to counterattack.

Emperor Marcus Aurelius erected the first major stone fortifications around the empire's capital city in the third century CE. Known as the Aurelian Walls, these defensive structures measured approximately 13 feet (4 m) wide at their base and, initially, reached approximately 20 feet (6 m) high, but later emperors built them to heights of nearly 66 feet (20 m). The walls were reinforced with concrete cores. Every 98 feet (30 m) there stood a rectangular tower, known as a **battlement**, designed to hold troops and artillery, such as the ballista. (The Latin word *ballista* comes from the Greek *ballo*, meaning "to throw," and is the root of the word "ballistic," relating to projectiles.) The ballista was what's known as a torsion weapon because its power derived from the torque built up as a result of tension in the weapon's arms. It resembled a large crossbow but with two horizontal arms, which provided enough force to hurl large spears known as bolts. The Aurelian Walls remain remarkably intact even today, in part because they continued to be used in battle up until the nineteenth century, but also because of their exceptional strength of materials and design.

The fortifications built by the Romans stood even after the empire eroded. Those people living on the frontier of Europe moved into the structures that had been left, sometimes adopting and improving them to fit their own needs. The Franks, who occupied many of the forts that had been built during Roman wars of conquest, built interior fortifications into a corner of the existing fort to serve as a secondary line of defense. There they would build a central citadel, or keep, as well as structures essential to the operation and defense of the town, such as a garrison, quarters for the constable, a church, and a well. However, such fortified towns were unusual in Europe in the years preceding the Crusades, and most Christians still relied on simple wooden palisades for protection.

FORTIFIED CITIES OF THE MUSLIM WORLD

Because many of the world's oldest civilizations had settled in the Near East and fortified their homelands for millennia before the rise of Islam, the Muslim world benefited from the existence of battle-tested defenses already in place during their period of expansion. Among these was Jerusalem, the control of which was the primary objective throughout the Crusades. Jerusalem had been fortified since the Bronze Age, and as it changed hands among such cultures as the Jews, the Babylonians, the Romans, and eventually the Muslims, it benefited from a series of expansions, improvements, and innovations.

By the time of the Crusades, Jerusalem was heavily fortified, protected by a series of semiconcentric walls that corresponded to periods in which the city expanded. These walls were each protected by massive square towers, which had been rebuilt, reinforced, and improved over centuries, as well as reinforced gates, many of which were doubled as a second layer of defense. Jerusalem was dominated by the citadel, which housed the city's major political, economic, and religious structures. In the event of a siege, those in control of Jerusalem could recede farther and farther into the maze of the city's defenses; should one sector fall, there remained several fallback positions, which in effect made the siege of one city a series of sieges to be won.

CRUSADER CASTLES

The Crusaders, largely used to simple defenses made primarily of wood back in Europe, must have been impressed and intimidated by the high, reinforced stone fortifications of the old cities of the Near East. The Crusaders would have to improvise more advanced siege techniques than they had been using in the West (see chapter 5), and following the capture of Jerusalem after the First Crusade, they embarked on construction projects to erect larger, stronger fortifications in order to repel the inevitable Muslim counterattack and consolidate their control of the Holy Land.

In the wake of their first expedition into the Holy Land, the Crusaders further reinforced the cities now under their command, including Jerusalem, Cairo, Antioch, and Acre, with larger walls built in concentric circles and protected by round towers instead of square ones. Round towers had been in use since the Roman Empire but did not find widespread application until the Crusades. While square towers are easier to build and afford a greater amount of usable interior space for housing garrisoned soldiers, weapons, and supplies, round towers offer greater resistance to siege techniques such as **sapping** and projectile attack. Much like an arch can support more weight in a wall, a round tower can absorb greater impact without breaking by distributing the force throughout the structure. Round towers also have a greater chance of deflecting a projectile fired at an oblique angle.

The Crusaders also built new castles in order to oversee and protect the less developed regions within their newly captured lands. Among these is Krak des Chevaliers (Castle of the Knights) in Syria, which remains largely intact today and is recognized by the worldwide heritage protection agency UNESCO as the best-preserved testament to the cultural interplay at work during the Crusades. Krak des Chevaliers was built starting in 1142 by the Knights of St. John, otherwise known as the Hospitallers. The castle consists of two concentric walls, separated by a moat, both of which feature round towers.

Krak des Chevaliers (Castle of the Knights) in Syria represented the pinnacle of fortification technology during the Crusades.

The inner wall, 10 feet (3 m) thick, is raised to overlook the outer. The castle itself was built on top of a ridge, granting it an exceptional vantage point over the surrounding countryside. The Krak des Chevaliers was designed to accommodate two thousand troops, one thousand horses, and enough supplies for the garrison to last for approximately five years before resupply.

Krak des Chevaliers proved a formidable fortress and survived several attempts to conquer it. In 1188, the mighty Muslim general Saladin besieged the castle and even captured its commander, whom he demanded order his troops within the castle to surrender. According to legend, the commander said just that to the soldiers under his command in Arabic, but afterward spoke in French and ordered them to fight until the last man. The Hospitallers maintained control of the castle until 1271, when it was lost to Muslim forces under Sultan Baybars I, who tricked the defenders into surrendering the castle by delivering a forged letter from their regional commander in Tripoli ordering them to leave.

The Siege of Constantinople

During the Muslim world's campaign of conquest in the seventh and eighth centuries, the Arab armies twice tried to capture Constantinople, Christianity's stronghold in the East and capital of the Byzantine Empire. Constantinople was situated on an elevated peninsula overlooking the Bosporus, the strait connecting the Black Sea with the Sea of Marmara and the Mediterranean, making it of extraordinary strategic value. Capturing the city would open the Eastern door into Europe. However, on both attempts, Constantinople repelled Muslim invaders, in part due to its strong fortifications.

Constantinople's fortifications blended superior materials, ingenious architecture, and natural defenses. Its first walls were built by Emperor Constantine (for whom the city was named) in the fourth century CE and completely enclosed the city. In 413, Emperor Theodosius improved Constantine's design, building a wall that stretched from one side of the peninsula to the other, completely sealing off the city from the mainland. When earthquakes damaged much of the wall in 447, the Byzantines rebuilt it and improved on it, adding an additional shorter, thinner wall known as the outer wall.

Thanks to its fortifications and the leadership of astute commanders, Constantinople was considered one of the best-defended cities in the known world. However, it seems its greatest threat came from within Christendom, the very religious group protecting it. In 1204, during the Fourth Crusade, Christian soldiers turned mutinous, laying siege to and plundering the city themselves. Constantinople never recovered from the assault, and in 1453 the city fell to the Muslim Ottoman Turks. Remains of Constantinople's walls still stand today, in what was renamed Istanbul by the Turks.

The improvement of fixed fortifications sparked a need for improved weapons called siege engines capable of circumventing them.

CHAPTER FIVE

Siege Warfare

The architectural exchange that occurred during the Crusades led to the rapid development of more impressive, secure fortresses, which only became more important as control of territory came to be decided less and less by pitched battles between large armies. As a result, the need for more sophisticated and powerful weaponry designed to isolate, attack, and eventually overtake these defensive positions became of the utmost importance. While one side battened down the hatches, the forces of the displaced side worked to implement new technologies to best their opponents. The result was a boom in siege warfare, especially in machines known as siege engines designed to damage or circumvent a fortress's walls.

BASIC SIEGE ENGINES

While the Crusades saw the fielding of massive siege engines, the practice of besieging a fortified area was not unique to the Crusades. For as long as humans have been building walls to protect something valuable—be it land, riches, or people—other humans have been working out ways to circumvent them. Sieges often took a long time, sometimes months or even years. The first Muslim siege of Constantinople, for example, lasted five years. In cases of stalemate, where direct attacks on a fortress were repelled, the attacking army was left to simply wait out the defenders, hoping to starve them into submission. Although the attackers often effectively isolated a fortress from the outside world by encircling it with earthen walls, fortresses often stockpiled supplies for just such an occasion, though sometimes besieged cities forced nonessential civilians out to face the enemy in order to reduce the demand for resources. The waiting game was not always advantageous to the besiegers either, as they also had to survive long encampments in poorly built battlefield structures, relying on their own fragile supply lines and a barren countryside for support. In these instances, sieges essentially became wars of attrition, with both sides suffering severe casualties. Attacking armies recognized the importance of hastening a siege and penetrating the fortress walls faster. Thus, ancient inventors began work on a variety of machines designed to do just that.

Generally speaking, there have been three ways of directly assaulting stationary defenses: going over, going under, and going through. Attackers often attempted to apply the most pressure on the defenders by utilizing the widest variety of techniques possible, which helped to divide the defenders' attention and thereby weaken the overall defense of a fortress. After all, defenders had to stop every possible entry into their stronghold, but attackers only needed one of several or even dozens of possible strategies to successfully defeat a fortress's defenses.

Perhaps the most straightforward way to enter a fortress was to force a way through. The simplest way of penetrating a defense was the sneak attack, in which armed forces would attempt to penetrate an area without notice, hoping to catch the defenders off guard. As civilizations came to organize larger armies and develop stronger means of defenses, however, the likelihood of a large force entering the area around a stronghold unnoticed grew slimmer. Attacking armies had to implement specially designed siege equipment to attack an enemy holed up behind steep walls. One of the oldest purpose-built siege engines was the battering ram, which dates back to prehistory. At its most basic, the battering ram consists of a tree trunk or large log propelled with force against a door, gate, or wall. During the Iron Age (approximately 1200 to 600 BCE), the battering ram was improved by the addition of a metal cap to increase its strength, weight, and durability, and a suspension system, which hoisted the ram onto a frame to support a heavier—and thus more powerful—ram. Most early suspended battering ram frames also included wheels to allow besieging soldiers to easily maneuver them to a target. By the Crusades, battering rams also included a protective cover, known as a cat, made of wood and dampened animal hides to protect the soldiers operating the ram from defenders' attacks, such as rocks, arrows, fire, and hot oil. Usually the cat could be separated from the ram and maneuvered on its own to serve as a mobile workspace for engineers working around the enemy walls.

The ram proved an effective siege engine until the end of the thirteenth century—approximately the end of the last crusade. However, the ram was a time-consuming method of destroying the enemy walls. Siege commanders looking for a simpler, faster way of surmounting defenses turned to a method known as the **escalade**. In this method, attackers climbed over the walls. The two most common siege engines designed to deliver troops over

The battering ram was one of the oldest siege engines, dating back to prehistory, designed to punch through doors, gates, and walls.

rather than through fortress walls were the ladder and the siege tower. Ladders had a few advantages over other siege engines. Because ladders were much simpler and required fewer resources to build than many other siege weapons, an attacking force could field a large number of siege ladders, presenting a greater number of potential points of entry and diverting the defenders' attention. They were also lighter, allowing a squad of troops to quickly carry them across an expanse. However, ladders were also very exposed to projectiles; ladder squads often had to rely on friendly archers to provide volleys of arrows to suppress the fire coming from the defenders. More often than not, soldiers scaling ladders only had their personal armor to rely on for protection. Furthermore, ladders' light weight was also a liability, as defending armies could simply topple them with hooks or the force of combined strength once the enemy reached a wall.

Siege engineers counteracted the weakness of the ladder with the siege tower. Also known as a belfry, the siege tower dates back to the Assyrian Empire, a warlike civilization that dominated Mesopotamia between the fourteenth and seventh centuries BCE. The siege tower was a protected mobile structure usually built higher than a fortress's walls. Inside the siege tower was a series of levels that soldiers could ascend by means of stairs or ladders. At the top of the tower was a drawbridge, which would drop down onto the battlements, allowing the soldiers inside to spill out. Like the cat that covered a battering ram, siege towers usually had wooden frames covered in wet animal hides to prevent

The siege tower, or belfry, was one of the most effective means of scaling a fortress's walls.

the defenders from setting fire to the tower. Some siege towers also included a platform for archers to fire down on defenders. Others, including that used by Godfrey's forces during the siege of Jerusalem in 1099, featured a battering ram designed to punch through outer walls before approaching a fortress's main wall.

Although the siege tower was more effective at scaling walls than ladders, no siege engine is perfect, and the tower likewise had its drawbacks. Siege towers were the heaviest and most complicated siege engines, which made building and transporting them difficult, a problem exacerbated by the vast distances the Christian armies had to travel to reach the Holy Land during the Crusades. During the Third Crusade, for example, the king of England, Richard the Lionhearted, had to construct his siege towers on the Mediterranean island of Cyprus before shipping them to mainland Palestine to complete their assembly.

Furthermore, siege towers' height coupled with their relatively small base made them top-heavy. Siege towers were only effective on flat terrain; traversing uneven land ran the risk of toppling the belfry. Some fortified cities and castles of the Crusades capitalized on this weakness and were either built on naturally rocky or otherwise rugged terrain, such as a hilltop or ridge, or purposefully made their surrounding land uneven by digging ditches or moats. In these cases, engineers within besieging armies had to literally level the field, such as by building an earthen causeway across a ditch or, in the case of the siege of Jerusalem in 1099, filling the ditch with stones.

COVERING FIRE

Rams, ladders, siege towers, and other methods of directly assaulting a fortress often faced a constant torrent of arrows, stones, and hot oil raining down from the parapets. Not only did this slow the progress of the siege engines, but it also cost the lives of soldiers and occasionally resulted in the destruction of the machines themselves. Commanders of besieging armies recognized the need to prevent defenders from harassing their troops in the first place. Armies occasionally fielded archers behind mobile wooden walls known as mantlets to protect siege engines with a volley of arrows, but their range was shorter, leaving them as exposed as the soldiers working on the walls. The more effective option was to employ artillery units operating larger, more powerfully ranged weapons.

Squad-operated heavy-ranged weapons had been in use for centuries before the Crusades. The Romans, for example, pioneered the ballista (mentioned in chapter 4), which saw some use in the Crusades. The ballista was a powerful antipersonnel weapon capable of skewering several troops unfortunate enough to be standing in a line, but it had little application against reinforced walls.

The catapult, also known as the mangonel or onager, was somewhat more flexible than the ballista in Crusader sieges, capable of targeting defending troops as well as damaging a fortress's walls. It was especially popular among the French armies. Like the ballista, the catapult was a torsion weapon originally

The catapult was an effective antipersonnel ballistic weapon, capable of hurling small projectiles a great distance.

designed centuries before the Crusades. The basic design of a catapult included an arm attached at one end to a wooden frame by a pivot that was under tension. Some catapults got their torque from a horizontal bar similar to that of a ballista, while others were powered by tightly wrapped cordage exerting pressure on the pivot. At the free end was a bowl large enough to hold a blunt projectile, such as a boulder. The arm was cocked in a horizontal position, usually by a winch, and when it was released, it would fling forward, stopping at a crossbar and hurling its projectile. The maximum range of a catapult was approximately 1,600 feet (488 m), well outside the range of an archer. Groups of catapults were used in conjunction with one another during the Crusades to deliver volleys of boulders.

Catapults were only marginally effective in sieges. Though they could be used against personnel as well as fixed defenses, they were somewhat weak, capable of firing only small projectiles with low velocity. This meant that they were capable of suppressing defenders but could not themselves penetrate fortified walls. For that task, the armies of the Crusades turned to the trebuchet.

The trebuchet, like the catapult and ballista, was a ballistic weapon; however, unlike its counterparts, the trebuchet did not rely on built-up torque to fire its projectiles. Rather, the trebuchet was based off a simple mechanical device, the lever. It consisted of a long beam with a sling on one end, a heavy counterbalance at the other, and a pivot between the two. The size of a trebuchet depended on the length of its arm and the size and weight of its counterweight, which scaled to accommodate various sizes of missiles, ranging from 85 pounds to 300 pounds (40–136 kilograms).

When preparing to fire a trebuchet, the sling end of the arm would be cranked back, with the sling resting on the ground toward the pivot. When the arm was released, the counterweight pulled on it, whipping the sling and lending rotational acceleration. At a certain point, the sling would release its projectile at a high trajectory. Although the trebuchet suffered from the same limitation of velocity as the catapult, the fact that trebuchets fired high into the air rather than directly at a target meant that their missiles would accelerate from the force of gravity and come crashing down. Modern reproductions of trebuchets seem to be able to cause damage similar to modern mortars, which made them the most powerful ballistic weapons available to the armies of the Crusades, capable of inflicting significant damage to wood and stone fortifications.

The trebuchet was developed in the twelfth century, and its strength quickly made it an asset to Crusaders besieging cities in the Holy Land. It proved so accurate and effective that it remained in use until the sixteenth century, well after gunpowder-based artillery had been widely introduced.

Send in the Sappers

Faced with the prospect of assaulting steep walls protected by hundreds or thousands of soldiers, many attacking armies opted to avoid the whole business altogether. Rather than face the whole of a fortress's might head on, they worked to erode its defenses from the bottom up, through mining. There were two common mining methods at work in Crusade sieges. In the first, a contingent of miners would use picks and hammers to chip away at the base of a wall. It seems the primary purpose of this attack was not to penetrate the wall but to weaken it somewhat before heavier siege engines were brought in.

The second method of mining was far more complicated and labor intensive. This method, known as sapping, began away from a fortress's walls, outside the range of ballistic attack if possible, under a protective, concealed cover. From here, the miners dug a subterranean tunnel leading just under the walls. If they managed to reach the walls, the miners would either begin to chip away at their stone base or deliberately set fire to their tunnel, causing a cave-in and hopefully weakening the wall or, better yet, bringing part of the wall down completely.

Besides the usual dangers associated with mining, sappers also faced detection from the defenders. Many fortresses were equipped with countermining technology. Usually this involved placing a bowl of water on top of the walls or in a previously dug mine and waiting to see if the water began rippling; if so, the defenders knew a mine was being dug. From there, they would dig their own mine to intercept the sappers. Most of the time, the defenders set fire to the tunnel, hoping to smoke the opposing miners out, but armed soldiers were occasionally sent into the mine to kill the attackers.

Standard armor during the Crusades included chainmail, pictured here on a French knight.

CHAPTER SIX

Implementing New Technology in the Later Crusades

For nearly two centuries after the First Crusade, animosity between Latin Christendom and Islam intermittently flared, and new Crusades were launched. Within a generation of the First Crusade, Christians sought to secure yet more territory in the Holy Land. The Islamic world in turn resisted further encroachment, blocking the spread of Crusader states and even pushing back to reclaim regions lost during the First Crusade. With each holy war, the armies of East and West further developed, implemented, and refined their tactics, fortifications, and equipment with mixed results.

CASTLES AND CONTROL

The key lesson of the First Crusade concerned the importance of winning and holding points of fixed defenses to secure control of the surrounding region. Beyond the religious significance of the Crusaders capturing Antioch and Jerusalem, the cities presented significant tactical advantages. Both sieges had been hard fought, and were it not for a fair amount of luck, the First Crusade would have likely been squashed by Muslim reinforcements marching from Egypt without ever setting foot inside Jerusalem. Although the Muslims lost their cities, they nevertheless benefited from the ability to determine the circumstances of a siege, as demonstrated by Jerusalem's governor ad-Daulah's advance warning of the Crusader armies' approach and his efforts to make the land surrounding the city as inhospitable to those armies as possible.

Although the First Crusade succeeded in its goal of capturing Jerusalem, the lasting success of Latin Christendom in the Holy Land had yet to be seen. The territories under Crusader control were still essentially isolated and vulnerable to counterattack, despite controlling two major cities, and all the achievement seemed to teeter on the edge of destruction. In 1101, Pope Pascal II called an expedition of Crusaders to try to secure more cities in the Holy Land and thereby extend Latin Christendom's network of control. Although the force was defeated in Asia Minor, the cities of Arsuf, Caesarea, Acre, Beirut, and Sidon were in Crusader hands by 1112. These victories served to establish control of the coast, which facilitated later expeditions by providing secure landing points for troops and supplies.

In order to expand the benefits of fixed fortifications throughout their newly won territory, the Crusaders built satellite states in the Holy Land. The armies of the First Crusade had benefited greatly from the fact that much of the land between Constantinople, Antioch, and Jerusalem was undefended wilderness. In fact, the success of the Crusaders' siege of Jerusalem depended in large part on the speed with which they could traverse Palestine with minimal harassment. This presented certain disadvantages, such as tiring out the force and causing a situation in which there was no secure route for supplies or escape, but it also meant that the Crusaders could set up around Jerusalem in advance of Muslim reinforcements from Egypt. The Christians, grateful for this fact, quickly went to work building a network of strongholds and outposts in the wilderness to prevent a future Muslim army from making use of the same advantage. Each fortress served as a buffer to another, such that an army could not approach a key city without first capturing or finding a way around a defended fortress.

Baldwin of Bouillon, who broke off from the main force of the First Crusade, began laying the groundwork for this web of fortifications when he captured the county of Edessa in Syria. Raymond of Saint-Gilles, who also separated from the main army of the First Crusade, traveled to Tripoli and established a state there. Meanwhile, Latin Christians built castles in Galilee in northern Palestine. At the center of these Crusader states was the Kingdom of Jerusalem, the crown of the Holy Land.

MUSLIM SUPREMACY

Despite the Crusaders' network of fortified cities and outposts, Muslim forces nevertheless chipped away at Latin Christendom's tenuous hold on its territories in the Holy Land. The extent of Christianity's control amounted to a long, narrow strip of land running north to south, caught between the Mediterranean Sea to the west and a number of mountain ranges to the east. Later Crusader attempts to capture Muslim cities to the east, such as Aleppo in Syria, failed. The geography of the region meant that the Crusader states were still vulnerable—a coordinated attack could effectively sever the narrow strip of land connecting their network.

In 1144, Muslim forces captured Edessa, the Europeans' northernmost place of power. By this point, the formerly fractured Islamic world had largely unified under the leadership of a Syrian named Nur al-Din. This loss of Edessa prompted a monk named St. Bernard of Clairvaux to begin preaching for a Second Crusade, which Pope Eugene II formally ordered in 1145. However, the European armies floundered, and Nur al-Din went on to capture Damascus in 1154. Between 1169 and 1171, the Fatimid caliphate handed their territories over to Nur al-Din as well.

Nur al-Din's rule not only helped unify most of the Islamic world but also served to isolate and surround the Crusader states of the Holy Land, laying the groundwork for the Muslims' most dynamic and shrewd military leader, Saladin, to launch an offensive in 1187. Saladin managed to draw the Crusader army garrisoned in Jerusalem out from the security of their fortress, crushing them in an open battle. By the end of the year, Saladin captured practically all the territory in the Kingdom of Jerusalem, including Jerusalem itself. Unlike the Crusaders after their victory in the First Crusade, Saladin permitted the commander of Jerusalem, Balian of Ibelin, his forces, and the residents of the city to leave relatively peacefully.

This reversal of fortunes proved so shocking to the papacy that the sitting pope, Urban III, allegedly died after hearing the news. His successor, Gregory VIII, summoned the armies of Europe to again mobilize for the Third Crusade (1189–1192). By that point, the Muslims under Saladin had managed to repel sieges. An interesting development around this period involved the use of a large hook designed to catch the end of a battering ram and topple it. Although the Crusaders failed to retake Jerusalem, they managed to capture Acre on the Mediterranean coast and secure an agreement with Saladin to allow Christian pilgrims to travel to and enter the Holy City.

COMBATTING CAVALRY

Saladin's conquest of Jerusalem owed to his ability to draw Crusader forces out of the city. In a pitched battle, Muslim cavalry tactics proved superior to Crusader knights. Ranged attacks followed by retreat on horseback allowed Muslim forces to pick off Christian warriors easily. Furthermore, the heavily armored Christian knights could not make full use of their devastating charge because the more lightly outfitted Muslims could outrun and outmaneuver them.

Faced with this problem, French Crusaders decided to implement a relatively new technology that would help give them an advantage against mounted Muslim archers: the crossbow. First developed in the technologically advanced city-states of the Italian peninsula around the turn of the millennium, the crossbow consisted of a short bow oriented horizontally on a short wooden stock with a groove to hold a missile, known as a bolt. The crossbow string was held in place by a hook known as a sear, which released when the operator pulled a trigger. Many crossbows also featured a hand-operated mechanical crank and stirrup in which a bowman placed his foot to facilitate the draw of the string up to the sear. Although the crossbow required more strength to initially cock than a bow, the fact that it stored its mechanical energy until the crossbowman fired meant that its bolt could fly faster, farther, and with greater penetrating power than an arrow fired from a conventional bow. It also demanded less skill from its user and offered greater precision, allowing a crossbowman to take careful aim without constantly struggling against the weight of the draw. The crossbow was so effective that the Second Lateran Council, convened by the pope in 1139, outlawed its use against Christians, calling it a "murderous art … which is hateful to God." Despite this moral prohibition, the Latin Church permitted its soldiers to use crossbows against Muslim armies during the Crusades.

The Children's Crusade

In the summer of 1212, Crusader fervor again spread through Europe. This time, the volunteer army consisted not of knightly nobles but of young children. Known as the *pueri* (Latin for "young boy"), the child Crusaders organized around a shepherd boy called Stephen of Cloyes, who in May 1212 participated in a procession through Chartres, France, requested by Pope Innocent III to pray for the success of Crusaders in Spain. Stephen, along with a number of fellow shepherds, sparked a wave of enthusiasm among members of their generation. The procession lasted for over a month, during which time Stephen and his followers traveled across France. By late June, their numbers swelled, ranging from fifteen thousand to thirty thousand. Although the French king ordered Stephen to disband his followers, groups of pueri continued to travel through central Europe.

Crusader enthusiasm spread to Germany, where a boy named Nicholas of Cologne again organized the pueri and suggested that they travel to the Holy Land to reclaim Jerusalem and the true cross on which Jesus was crucified. Both had been lost to the Muslims at the end of the Fourth Crusade. Drawing a parallel to the Israelite Exodus from Egypt, Nicholas said that the Mediterranean Sea would part before them, and that they could march straight into Jerusalem.

Despite their zeal, none of the Crusaders reached the Holy Land. Nicholas led his "soldiers" across the Alps and into Genoa, Italy, but to their surprise, the Mediterranean did not part, nor could they find a ship willing to take them to the Holy Land. With nowhere to go, the child Crusaders dispersed. Many may have traveled on to Rome to request that their Crusader vows be annulled, while others sought passage to Marseille, France. Those that remained in Genoa likely found work, either willingly or as slaves. Whatever path they took, few of the children returned home alive, as the majority died of starvation, thirst, or drowning during their travels.

Cavalry units were widely employed on the battlefield as recently as World War I. Here, French lancers prepare to leverage their mounts' speed and power to charge retreating enemy troops.

CHAPTER SEVEN

Crusader Tech Today

Nearly a millennium after Pope Urban II called for the First Crusade, the Near East, particularly the holy places situated in the Levant, continue to be a hotbed for conflict. Throughout the centuries, control of the Middle East has shifted among several different powers, just as it had during the Crusades. Today, terrorist groups preaching a perverted form of Islam continue to summon "true believers" to wage a renewed war of religion.

Although the face of war may have changed since the First Crusade, war itself never changes. Mounted knights may have stopped charging across the Holy Land, but in their place are elite soldiers wielding sophisticated technology transported rapidly across the battlefield in heavily armored vehicles.

CAVALRY IN MODERN WAR

Although knighthood survives largely as a ceremonial honor in European countries, the need for heavily armored, fast-moving troops in battle is as strong today as it was during the Crusades. Horses have played an important role on the battlefield as recently as World War I (1914–1918), considered to be the first "modern" war. Although the automobile was invented before World War I, and the armored tank was introduced during the war, the armies that fought continued to employ horses because they could travel across terrain those crude machines couldn't, especially the perpetually muddy battlefields that proved too troublesome for the wheels and tracks of cars and tanks. The British military alone counted nearly half a million horses in service during one year of the Great War. Half of those were used as supply horses, transporting everything from ammunition to artillery pieces across central Europe, and over seventy-five thousand were still used as armed cavalry forces.

Tragically, the horrors of modern war were not unknown to the animals. Gun and artillery fire, malnutrition, injuries, and exposure to harsh elements claimed the lives of eight million horses globally during World War I. Automobile technology advanced significantly in the wake of the war. All-terrain vehicles such as jeeps, motorcycles, and trucks, as well as improved tanks all but replaced the need for horses in warfare after 1918. Fortunately, most military horses today are used only for ceremonial purposes, serving as mounts for officers during parades.

While the use of horses in war has declined significantly since the early twentieth century, many modern militaries still count cavalry divisions within their ranks of fighting units. Instead of lancers riding armor-clad horses, these units consist of multiton armored troop transports topped with powerful weapons. A variety of these vehicles are known as armored personnel carriers (APCs). Despite being packed with sophisticated modern technology, at their core the APCs are designed to provide similar tactical advantages as the knights of the Crusades: APCs are designed to carry a squad of troops across an active battlefield more quickly and relatively safely than those soldiers could move on foot. To that end, many APCs feature dropdown hatches in their rear to allow soldiers to board and disembark quickly in the heat of battle.

APCs are like multi-tools in the arsenals of modern militaries, capable of filling a variety of roles depending on the way they are outfitted. This means that there are a wide variety of APC designs. Generally speaking, there are two kinds of APCs: wheeled and tracked. Wheeled APCs tend to be lighter, faster, and capable to traversing more varied terrain. Tracked APCs are slower, but they are able to carry a greater weight, be it in armament, armor, or personnel. APCs, as their name suggests, feature reinforced steel or lighter-weight aluminum armor capable of resisting small arms fire, but many also feature sophisticated ventilation systems that make them resistant to "dirty" biological attack and even nuclear weapons. Some APCs travel unarmed, acting as cargo carriers or battlefield ambulances, but many feature weapons systems, from antipersonnel automatic grenade launchers and .50-caliber machine guns up to antiaircraft missile launchers.

Despite the prevalence of APCs on the battlefield, there are still some horses that continue to see combat, though in very limited applications. Some elite special forces units, particularly those trained to fight in mountainous terrain, get around not on advanced machines like APCs but on horses. The United States Army, for example, generally recognized as the most technologically advanced military in the world, hosts the Marine Corps Mountain Warfare Training Center in the Sierra Nevada Mountains in California. There, soldiers from a variety of special forces units undergo a fifteen-day training course detailing how to maneuver on horseback as well as how to find horses suited to travel while abroad. Horses are ideally suited to the rough, remote, and mountainous terrain of places like Afghanistan, which for years has been the focus of America's counterterrorism operations. They can quickly and quietly traverse uneven ground, requiring only feed and water. Vehicles, even all-terrain vehicles, can only travel so far before requiring refueling and maintenance, and because isolated battlefields tend not to feature gas stations or mechanic shops, these vehicles need established lines—roads—to provide those materials. As terrorist groups retreat farther and farther into inhospitable terrain, the benefits of horses come to outweigh those of vehicles.

FROM CHAIN MAIL TO BULLETPROOF VESTS

Following the Crusades, the mail armor favored by knights was slowly replaced by solid sections of armor, known as plate armor, which became less expensive as metalworking techniques improved. By the fourteenth century, whole sets of plate armor, known today as the "suit of armor," replaced mail. However, with the implementation of gunpowder artillery and personal firearms capable of penetrating armor, suits of plate armor lost their relevance on the battlefield. In the sixteenth and seventeenth centuries, armor that was thick enough to resist a bullet proved too heavy and cumbersome to be worn on the battlefield. Nevertheless, the ability to protect a soldier from projectiles has been of concern for the world's militaries, leading to the development of "bulletproof vests." Although the range, accuracy, and power of firearms has continued to improve, personal armor similar to that worn by the Crusaders seems to be making a comeback today. However, modern personal armor is made not of solid iron or steel but of plastic.

During World War II (1939–1945), the British company Wilkinson Sword developed the "flak jacket," a vest designed to protect Royal Air Force crews from shrapnel, metal splinters that form when an artillery round explodes. (The word "flak" is a shortening of the German word *Fliegerabwehrkanone*, which means "aircraft-defense canon," the weapon the vest was designed to protect against.) The flak jacket was inspired by an early "bulletproof" vest prototype from the American Civil War and consisted of solid steel plates sewn into a nylon body. These flak jackets afforded the pilots some additional protection while only partially restricting their freedom of movement, but flak jackets were not true "bulletproof" armor. Although effective at stopping fragments of shrapnel, which are larger and travel at a lower velocity than bullets, the flak jacket could not stop a bullet. Flak jackets were never incorporated into infantry units because of their weight.

During the Korean War (1950–1953), the United States military improved on the flak jacket by removing the bulky steel plates and opting for multiple dense layers of nylon, which cut the weight down to 8 pounds (3.6 kg). When the improved flak jacket was

A salesman demonstrates the stopping power of the bulletproof vest to a policeman.

widely introduced, an army study found that it reduced shrapnel wounds to the parts of the body covered by the vest by 70 percent. However, as before, the vest was only antifragmentary, protecting against shrapnel but still vulnerable to ballistics.

A truly bulletproof vest would not be developed until the second half of the twentieth century. In 1965, the chemical company DuPont synthesized a plastic known as Kevlar. Initially designed to reduce the weight of tires, the company soon realized that it was not only lighter but better at stopping bullets than the nylon being used in flak jackets. In 1975, the military started using Kevlar in its flak jackets. Today, bulletproof vests made of Kevlar and other similar plastics are used by soldiers, police officers, and others who work in places where gunshot wounds are common.

Kevlar's strength derives both from its regular parallel arrangement on the molecular level and the way individual fibers are woven together to form an interconnected network—interestingly, similar to the metal rings of medieval mail. Similar to its nylon predecessors, Kevlar vests include between sixteen and twenty-four layers of material, with more layers offering greater stopping power. When a bullet hits the first few layers of a Kevlar vest, its own force causes it to mushroom out. This creates a larger projectile whose force is greatly reduced by it being spread out across a wider, blunter surface area. The weave of a Kevlar vest helps to disperse this force and ultimately (hopefully) stops it (although getting shot while wearing a bulletproof vest still tends to knock the wind out of the wearer and leaves a nasty bruise). Alone, a Kevlar vest is rated to protect against a 9mm bullet fired from a handgun; higher-caliber bullets fired from larger firearms tend to penetrate the vest. However, many modern bulletproof vests also feature pockets designed to hold hardened ceramic plates for additional protection.

While the Crusades were a time of fierce fighting and division, they also enabled new inventions and combat techniques to be developed. These innovations in turn have evolved into improved inventions and practices. No doubt they will continue to be adapted as the years and centuries progress.

Modern cavalry forces consist of armored personnel carriers designed to move troops around a battlefield quickly and safely.

The Sharksuit

A modern type of armor similar to the metal chain mail worn by the Crusaders continues to find use today, but instead of protecting knights from slashes and pierces on the dusty battlefields of the Near East, this armor is most at home in the shark-infested waters of the open sea. In 1978, a marine biologist named Jeremiah Sullivan introduced the sharksuit to protect aquarium workers, marine biologists, and other divers researching sharks from bites. Like medieval mail, the sharksuit is composed of thousands of interlocking metal rings and comes in a variety of protective pieces, including tunics, sleeves, gloves, pants, booties, and hoods. However, these modern rings are much smaller and are made of more sophisticated metals, stainless steel and titanium, designed to prevented the sharp, serrated teeth of sharks from penetrating.

Opposite: A marine biologist designed the Neptunic sharksuit to protect divers from shark bites. This invention means that mail is more likely to be found exploring the depths of the ocean than on the arid battlefields of the Near East!

GLOSSARY

apocalyptic Describing the final destruction of the entire world as prophesied in the Book of Revelation in the Christian Bible and the Quran of Islam.

Ark of the Covenant A sacred artifact containing the slabs on which the Ten Commandments were etched.

battlement The section at the top of a wall with regularly spaced openings for defenders to shoot through.

caliph The chief ruler of Islam considered to be the inheritor to Muhammad.

Church of the Holy Sepulchre A church originally built by the mother of the Roman emperor Constantine in the fourth century CE over the site traditionally thought to be the place of Jesus Christ's crucifixion and tomb.

citadel A stronghold within a fortified castle or city, usually built on higher ground, to serve as a fallback position in the event of a siege and designed to protect the major religious and political structures of an area.

Crusade A war commenced by the Latin Church for religious purposes; in the eleventh, twelfth, and thirteenth centuries, the Latin Church called for a series of such wars against the Islamic world.

ecumenical Involving a number of Christian churches.

escalade A siege tactic in which soldiers of the attacking army attempt to scale the walls of a castle or city.

feudalism The predominant political system of medieval Europe in which the king distributed lands to nobles in exchange for loyalty and a pledge to provide military aid when called on; the nobles in turn exchanged parcels of their land to a class of professional soldiers known as knights, who in turn allowed peasants known as serfs to live on and work the land.

heretical Describing a belief or opinion that is contrary to what is generally accepted.

Holy Land A region in modern-day Palestine and Israel with religious significance for Judaism, Christianity, and Islam, particularly the city of Jerusalem.

infidel A nonbeliever; used by both Christians and Muslims during the Crusades to describe members of the opposing religion.

Islam A monotheistic faith believed to have been revealed to the Prophet Muhammad by Allah, or God; translates as "submission" to the will of God. Adherents of Islam are known as Muslims.

jihad The concept of "war" or "struggle" in Islam against nonbelievers.

Latin Christianity The branch of Christianity that grew out of the Western Roman Empire and which derives its authority and doctrine from the leadership of the pope of Rome. Historically, it used Latin as the language of its liturgy.

Levant Countries of the eastern Medinterranean region.

lilia Sharpened stakes hidden in pits covered with leaves or dirt.

mail A type of flexible armor characterized by a number of interlocking metal rings.

sapping A siege technique in which an attacking army seeks to weaken the foundation of a wall, either by picking away at it directly or building a mine underneath which is then imploded.

siege A military tactic in which an attacking enemy surrounds a castle, city, or other fortified place in hopes of capturing it, either by cutting off the target's supplies and forcing surrender or by assault.

siege engine A device designed to penetrate or overcome the walls of a castle, fort, or city during a siege.

stimuli Small sharpened stakes driven into the ground at an angle with pointed metal barbs.

stirrups A pair of loops attached to either side of a horse's saddle with a flat base to support a rider's feet.

BIBLIOGRAPHY

Abels, Richard. "Timeline for the Crusades and Christian Holy War to c. 1360." United States Naval Academy. Accessed June 17, 2016. http://www.usna.edu/Users/history/abels/hh315/crusades_timeline.htm.

"Armor and Shields." Medieval Warfare. Accessed June 17, 2016. http://www.medievalwarfare.info/armour.htm.

Asbridge, Thomas. *The Crusades: The Authoritative History of the War for the Holy Land*. New York: HarperCollins, 2010.

Black, Annetta, and Kristen Cunningham, eds. "Krak des Chevaliers: Ruins of the Crusaders' Headquarters." Atlas Obscura. Accessed June 17, 2016. http://www.atlasobscura.com/places/krack-des-chevaliers.

Brown, Elizabeth A.R. "Feudalism." *Encyclopedia Britannica*. Accessed June 17, 2016. http://www.britannica.com/topic/feudalism.

"Crac des Chevaliers and Qal'at Salah El-Din." UNESCO World Heritage List. Accessed June 17, 2016. http://whc.unesco.org/en/list/1229.

Department of Medieval Art and the Cloisters. "The Crusades (1095–1291)." Heilbrunn Timeline of Art History. Accessed June 17, 2016. http://www.metmuseum.org/toah/hd/crus/hd_crus.htm.

Dickson, Gary. "Children's Crusade." *Encyclopedia Britannica*. Accessed June 17, 2016. http://www.britannica.com/event/Childrens-Crusade.

Edge, David, and John Miles Paddock. *Arms and Armor of the Medieval Knight: An Illustrated History of Weaponry in the Middle Ages*. New York: Crescent Books, 1996.

The Editors of Encyclopedia Britannica. "Bulletproof Vest." *Encyclopedia Britannica*. Accessed June 17, 2016. http://www.britannica.com/technology/bulletproof-vest.

—. "Knight." *Encyclopedia Britannica*. Accessed June 17, 2016. http://www.britannica.com/topic/knight-cavalryman.

—. "Nur al-Din." *Encyclopedia Britannica*. Accessed June 17, 2016. http://www.britannica.com/biography/Nur-al-Din.

—. "Templar." *Encyclopedia Britannica*. Accessed June 17, 2016. http://www.britannica.com/topic/Templars.

—. "Thermopylae." *Encyclopedia Britannica*. Accessed June 17, 2016. http://www.britannica.com/place/Thermopylae.

Halsall, Paul. "Fulk of Chartres: The Capture of Jerusalem, 1099." Internet Medieval Sourcebook. Accessed June 17, 2016. http://legacy.fordham.edu/halsall/source/fulk2.asp.

"Hoplite." *Encyclopedia Britannica*. Accessed June 17, 2016. http://www.britannica.com/topic/hoplite.

ICEJ News. "The Significance of Jerusalem to Christians." International Christian Embassy Jerusalem, June 2, 2011. http://int.icej.org/news/commentary/significance-jerusalem-christians.

"Islamic Warfare." University of Michigan. Accessed June 17, 2016. http://www.umich.edu/~eng415/topics/war/islamic_warfare.html.

"Jeremiah Sullivan: A Legacy of Art and Science." Jeremiah Sullivan.com. Accessed June 17, 2016. http://www.jeremiahsullivan.com.

Kaufmann, J. E., and H. W. Kaufmann. *The Medieval Fortress: Castles, Forts and Walled Cities of the Middle Ages*. Cambridge, MA: De Capo Press, 2004.

Koerner, Brendan. "Flak Jackets vs. Bulletproof Vests: What's the Difference?" *Slate*. Accessed June 17, 2016. http://www.slate.com/articles/news_and_politics/explainer/2004/11/flak_jackets_vs_bulletproof_vests.html.

Phillips, Jonathan. "The Crusades: A Complete History." History Today, May 2015. http://www.historytoday.com/jonathan-phillips/crusades-complete-history.

Reid, Chip. "Inside the Horseback Training for U.S. Special Forces." CBS News, May 25, 2015. http://www.cbsnews.com/news/inside-the-horseback-training-for-u-s-special-forces.

Rogerson, Barnaby. *The Last Crusaders: The Hundred-Year Battle for the Center of the World*. New York: The Overlook Press, 2010.

"Sharksuits." Neptunic. Accessed June 17, 2016. http://neptunic.com/products/sharksuits.

"The Significance of Jerusalem in Judaism." Israel and Judaism Studies. Accessed June 17, 2016. http://www.ijs.org.au/Jerusalem-a-Jewish-Perspective/default.aspx.

"Sunnis and Shia: Islam's Ancient Schism." BBC News, January 4, 2016. http://www.bbc.com/news/world-middle-east-16047709.

Tanner, Norman P. "Second Lateran Council - 1139 A.D." Papal Encyclicals. Accessed June 17, 2016. http://www.papalencyclicals.net/Councils/ecum10.htm.

Viollet-Le-Duc, E. *Annals of a Fortress: Twenty-Two Centuries of Siege Warfare*. Mineola, NY: Dover Publications, 2007.

Wasson, Donald L. "The Army of Alexander the Great." Ancient History Encyclopedia, April 4, 2014. http://www.ancient.eu/article/676.

Whalen, Brett Edward. *Dominion of God: Christendom and Apocalypse in the Middle Ages*. Cambridge, MA: Harvard University Press, 2009.

"Who Were the Real War Horses of WWI?" BBC. Accessed June 17, 2016. http://www.bbc.co.uk/guides/zp6bjxs.

FURTHER INFORMATION

Books

Asbridge, Thomas. *The Crusades: The Authoritative History of the War for the Holy Land*. New York: HarperCollins, 2010.

Edge, David, and John Miles Paddock. *Arms and Armor of the Medieval Knight: An Illustrated History of Weaponry in the Middle Ages*. New York: Crescent Books, 1996.

Kaufmann, J. E., and H. W. Kaufmann. *The Medieval Fortress: Castles, Forts and Walled Cities of the Middle Ages*. Cambridge, MA: De Capo Press, 2004.

Websites

The Crusades

http://history-world.org/crusades.htm

This website includes articles on major topics of the Crusades, including overviews of the First and Third Crusades, a biography of the Muslim commander Saladin, and an account of Saladin's capture of Jerusalem.

History Today: The Crusades: A Complete History

http://www.historytoday.com/jonathan-phillips/crusades-complete-history

This website explains the Crusades in compelling detail. Explore exceptional high-quality, full-color scans of contemporary tapestries, maps, and portraits, as well as later visual source materials, that are sprinkled throughout the article. Its clickable outline format is easy to navigate and organizes a wealth of material.

Internet Medieval Sourcebook: Selected Sources: The Crusades
http://legacy.fordham.edu/halsall/sbook1k.asp
This website, hosted by Fordham University, is an outstanding collection of primary source material from the Crusades.

Videos

Crash Course History: The Crusades
http://www.youtube.com/watch?v=XOzudTQelzI
The popular YouTube channel Crash Course video on the Crusades succinctly explains the causes, events, and effects of the Crusades while helping to dispel some of the misinformation that has grown up around the wars over the centuries.

***Kingdom of Heaven* (2005)**
This film, directed by Ridley Scott and starring Orlando Bloom, Ghassan Massoud, Eva Green, and Jeremy Irons, depicts the events of the Second Crusade and Saladin's siege of Jerusalem. Although the movie fictionalizes many details of the lives of historical characters, it nevertheless accurately presents many of the story's "broad strokes" as well as the weapons, armor, tactics, and fortifications from the Crusader era. Rated R for violence and warfare.

INDEX

Page numbers in **boldface** are illustrations. Entries in **boldface** are glossary terms.

ABOUT THE AUTHOR

Andrew Coddington studied English, writing, and classics at Canisius College. He has written a number of books for Cavendish Square on a variety of topics, including history and ancient cultures and religions. He lives in Buffalo, New York, with his wife and dog.